Table of Contents

Now that you have these questions to help you get started, there are few factors which are important to implement before, starting reflection for an effective and positive outcome. 112

WELCOME TO THE STORY BEHIND THE COVER

The cover of Inspirational and Empowering a Holistic Journey, Personal Reflections on Life's Lessons and the Path to Growth Is a heartfelt invitation into a journey of self- discovery and personal growth. The hands gently releasing vibrant butterflies symbolize the beautiful process of letting go. Just as a butterfly emerges from its cocoon, so do we grow and transform when we release our fears and embrace life's lessons. Each butterfly, unique in color, represents the diverse experiences and insights that shape our lives, reminding use that every life lessons, quote, or message has its own unique value and beauty. The white background signifies a fresh, a blank canvas on which we paint our life's journey.

INSPIRATIONAL AND EMPOWERING LIFE LESSONS, A HOLISTIC JOURNEY

PERSONAL REFLECTIONS ON LIFE LESSONS AND THE PATH TO GROWTH

KRISTINA ALAVANJA

INTRODUCTION

Life is an endless journey of learning and growth, a voyage filled with life lessons and messages that shape our understanding of the world and ourselves. This book is a collection of such lessons and messages, drawn from my own life experiences. It is my hope that these insights will inspire and motivate you, sparking a positive transformation in your life.

Every life lesson carries a message with a profound meaning, regardless of its size or complexity. Just as life experiences come in waves of varying sizes, so too do these lessons and messages. Some are like small waves, manageable and with minimal impact on our lives. Others are like huge waves, overwhelming and challenging to navigate, yet survivable and often leading to the most significant growth.

What was the hardest life lesson you've ever learned? Were you able to decipher the message behind it? There are times when we feel like we're drowning in a massive wave, believing that survival is impossible. Yet, in the end, we often find that we can survive, learn valuable lessons, and understand the messages perfectly. What seems impossible can, with time, become a positive force in our lives.

Life lessons are the core insights or wisdom we gain from our experiences. They are the profound truths we learn through living, which fundamentally shape our understanding of life. These lessons often stem from significant events or milestones in our lives, such as overcoming a challenge, experiencing a failure, or achieving a long-sought goal.

Messages, on the other hand, are the specific interpretations or meanings we derive from our experiences. They are the takeaways, the 'moral of the story,' if you will. Messages are often more specific and situational than life lessons.

Life lessons and messages are interconnected. Messages often lead to life lessons. As we go through different experiences, we interpret specific messages from each situation. Over time, these messages accumulate and contribute to our overall understanding of life, forming our life lessons.

PEACE AMIDST CHAOES

"In the relentless hustle of life, we often find ourselves constantly on the move, juggling numerous tasks. Amidst this whirlwind, it becomes crucial to hit pause and carve out moments of tranquility for ourselves. Taking a break is not merely an act of leisure, but a fundamental necessity for our overall wellbeing and inner peace. It's about immersing ourselves in what brings us joy, what kindles our happiness. It's about living for ourselves in those moments, breathing in the freshness of life, and momentarily setting aside the stress and worries.

Being present in the moment is an art that we must all learn to master. It's a conscious act of appreciating the now, of soaking in the essence of our existence. If we let life pass us by without these moments of pause, we risk not only our happiness but also our health.

So, let's learn to appreciate being in the moment. Let's understand that our lives are not just about doing, but also about being. Let's remember to take a break, to enjoy life, and most importantly, to live for ourselves in those moments."

The Hustle of Life: In our fast-paced world, we often find ourselves caught up in a whirlwind of tasks and responsibilities. This constant hustle can leave us feeling overwhelmed and stressed. It's important to remember that amidst this chaos, we have the power to create moments of peace and tranquillity.

The Power of Pause: Taking a break is not just about rest, it's about rejuvenation. It's about stepping away from the hustle and bustle, even if just for a moment, to reconnect with ourselves. These moments of pause allow us to breathe, to reflect, and to regain our balance.

Joy and Happiness: During these moments of pause, we can immerse ourselves in activities that bring us joy and happiness. Whether it's reading a book, taking a walk-in nature, or simply enjoying a cup of tea, these activities can help us relax and recharge.

Being Present: Being present in the moment is an art. It's about fully experiencing the here and now, without dwelling on the past or worrying about the future. It's about appreciating the beauty of the present moment and the joy it brings.

Health and Wellbeing: Our mental health and wellbeing are just as important as our physical health. By taking breaks and being present in the moment, we not only enhance our happiness but also our health. It's a reminder that self-care should be a priority, not a luxury.

Doing vs Being: Often, we get so caught up in 'doing' that we forget about 'being'. Our lives are not just about accomplishing tasks, but also about experiencing moments. It's about being present, being mindful, and being in tune with ourselves.

In conclusion, finding peace amidst chaos is about taking breaks, immersing ourselves in joy, being present, prioritizing our health, and balancing 'doing' with 'being'. It's a reminder that amidst the hustle of life, we can create moments of peace and tranquillity. So, take a break, enjoy the moment, and remember, you are more than just your tasks and responsibilities. You are a human being deserving of peace, joy, and happiness.

EMBRACING DIFFERECES: BEYOND CONFLICT

"People are complex beings with multifaceted personalities. There are times when we don't understand one another, when we can't connect, or when we find ourselves in conflict. Sometimes, we may even drive each other crazy, wishing we could change one or two personality traits of the other person.

It's crucial to understand that we can't change others - we can only change ourselves and how we react to others' opinions and situations. No matter how much we try to change someone or want someone to align with our beliefs, needs, and opinions, it's not possible - and it's not okay. We all have flaws. If you find that you can't live with someone's flaws, then it's important to start thinking about your next steps."

Embracing Differences: Embracing differences is about acknowledging and appreciating the diversity of human personalities. It's about understanding that each person is unique, with their own set of strengths, weaknesses, beliefs, and values. It's about respecting these differences, not trying to change them.

Conflict and Misunderstanding: Conflict and misunderstanding are often the result of differences in personality, beliefs, or values. Instead of viewing these differences as obstacles, we can see them as opportunities for growth and understanding. They challenge us to broaden our perspectives, develop empathy, and improve our communication skills.

Personal Change: While we can't change others, we can change ourselves. This involves adjusting our attitudes, behaviours, and reactions. It's about developing emotional intelligence, practicing patience, and learning to communicate effectively. Personal change is a journey of self-improvement and growth.

Acceptance: Acceptance is a key aspect of embracing differences. It's about accepting others for who they are, flaws and all. It's about understanding that nobody is perfect, and that's okay. Acceptance fosters understanding, reduces conflict, and promotes harmony.

Next Steps: If you find it difficult to live with someone's flaws, it's important to reflect on your feelings and consider your next steps. This could involve having an open and honest conversation, seeking professional advice, or making changes in your relationship.

In conclusion, embracing differences is not just about tolerating diversity, but about appreciating it. It's about learning from our conflicts, changing ourselves, accepting others, and taking appropriate steps when necessary. Remember, our differences don't divide us, they enrich u.

EMPATHY WALK

"We all experience painful life situations and carry hidden pain behind our smiles and sweet words. Not everyone will fit your standards or be a perfect match for you. You won't always like someone, for whatever reasons those might be.

Don't judge those who live their lives by different standards. They are not perfect, but neither are you. Judging is part of being human - our brains are wired to automatically form opinions about others without needing to have a conversation or get to know them.

There are times when we do get to know someone, when we do have a conversation, but our perceptions are still influenced by our beliefs, upbringing, self-perception, and societal standards.

Remember, understanding and empathy are key to navigating our complex human interactions."

Personal Anecdote: I remember when I was in my teens, I judged someone without really knowing them. This incident sparked a flurry of questions in my mind. Why do we judge? What do we gain from it? How does it make us feel? And how would the person feel if they knew they were being judged?

As the years passed, life became hectic and at times, painful. These experiences changed my perception about judging others. I realized the importance of understanding someone and having an open mind. I learned to be more careful with my thoughts and judgments.

This personal journey taught me a valuable lesson: We should strive not to judge others based on superficial impressions, but rather seek to understand them better. After all, everyone is fighting their own battles, and a little empathy can go a long way.

Psychology: has long studied the mechanisms behind how we judge others, our behavior and mind. Our judgments are often influenced by cognitive biases, which are systematic errors in thinking that affect the decisions and judgments that people make.

KEY BIASES

Confirmation Bias: We tend to pay more attention to information that confirms our existing beliefs and ignore information that challenges them.

Stereotyping: We often categorize people based on their group membership, and these categories can influence our judgments.

Halo Effect: Our overall impression of a person can influence our feelings and thoughts about their character.

Understanding these psychological factors can help us become more aware of our own judgment processes and strive to make more fair and balanced judgments.

Quote: Maya Angelou once said, "People will forget what you said, people will forget what you did, but people will never forget how you made them feel." This quote reminds us of the lasting impact of our actions and the importance of treating others with kindness and understanding.

NAVIGATING EXPERIENCES: PRACTICAL TIPS

Practice Mindfulness: Try to stay present in each moment instead of dwelling on the past or worrying about the future.

Journaling: Write down your thoughts and feelings. This can help you process your experiences and learn from them.

Seek Professional Help: If your memories are causing significant distress, consider seeking help from a mental health professional.

REFLECTIVE QUESTIONS

Can you recall a time when you learned a valuable lesson from a painful memory? How has this experienced shaped who you are today? What strategies can you use to better cope with painful memories in the future?

CHERISHED MOMENTS

Every moment we live becomes a memory, whether it's a joyful memory filled with fun, love, and laughter, or a painful memory filled with sorrow and struggle. Each moment should not just be lived, but also remembered, because every experience carries a lesson to be learned.

It's normal and natural that we may not wish to remember painful moments because they're too distressing. However, you can't escape the memories you've lived; it's important to confront them, no matter how painful or difficult they may be. These memories are a part of you and will always be. Now, it's up to you to decide how you will let them impact you."

The Power of Positive Memories: Think back to a time when you achieved a goal you had set for yourself. The joy and satisfaction you felt at that moment is a positive memory. Such memories serve as reminders of our capabilities and motivate us to strive for more.

Learning from Negative Memories: Consider a time when you faced a setback or failure. While the memory might be painful, it also taught you resilience. You learned that setbacks are a part of life and that it's okay to fail. Most importantly, you learned to pick yourself up and try again.

The Role of Forgiveness: Recall a time when someone wronged you. Holding onto the anger and resentment can be more harmful to you than to the person who wronged you. By choosing to forgive, you free yourself from the burden of these negative emotions.

Creating Meaningful Moments: Spending quality time with loved ones, enjoying a hobby, helping others, or simply taking a moment to appreciate the beauty around you - these are all ways to create meaningful moments. Make it a point to do at least one thing every day that brings you joy.

Reflective Questions: What is a positive memory that brings you joy whenever you think about it? Can you recall a painful memory from which you learned a valuable lesson? How has that lesson shaped your actions or decisions since then?

SELF- LOVE

Everyone has flaws. Everything in this life and this world has flaws; nothing is perfect. Even roses, which are so beautiful and used to symbolize love and romance, have thorns. They have imperfections, yet you find them beautiful, and you use them to show love to others. Why won't you see yourself as a beautiful rose with a thorn? Instead, you see yourself as someone who is damaged and someone who is not good or worth it. When you can find beauty in roses, you can surely find beauty in yourself, because that imperfect beauty is perfect because it's real.

The way you see yourself is the way others will see you. What you give is what you will receive. Remember, self-love is a journey, not a destination. Take your time and remember to be kind to yourself along the way.

Practical Tips: Daily Affirmations: Start each day by looking in the mirror and saying something positive to yourself. It could be something like, "I am worthy of love and kindness," or "I am proud of who I am."

Mindfulness Exercises: Spend a few minutes each day in quiet reflection. Focus on your breath, and let go of negative thoughts as they arise.

Self-Care Practices: Make time for activities that bring you joy and relaxation. This could be reading a book, taking a walk-in nature, or treating yourself to a Favorite meal.

Personal Anecdote: I remember a time when I struggled with self-acceptance. I was always comparing myself to others and felt like I was never good enough. One day, I came across a quote that changed my perspective. It said, ""Accept yourself, love yourself, and keep moving forward. If you want to fly, you have to give up what weighs you down." **Roy T. Bennett.**

This quote resonated with me, and I started to realize that I needed to love and accept myself just as I am, without any comparisons or judgments.

HONOUR CHOICE

We all deserve to be treated with respect. At times, it is hard to show respect due to different biases and beliefs, and challenging situations. However, it is important to show respect even in these situations, as it speaks volumes about your self-control, character, and reputation.

Respect is earned, not demanded. It's important to remember this and to treat others the way you want to be treated. Being a good person doesn't mean that you will always get the respect you deserve in return. You only have control over yourself and how you act. Not everyone will respect your opinion or feelings. It's important to know how to respond and when to walk away.

Earning Respect: In a group project, if a team member misses deadlines, instead of complaining, you have a respectful conversation with them about how their actions affect the team. "If you have a disagreement with a friend about his choices, it is important to respect those choices and him, even if you don't agree with the choices he makes."

Reciprocating Respect: In a debate, if someone raises their voice and makes personal attacks, you remain calm and continue to express your points respectfully.

Walking Away: When dealing with a rude customer who refuses to listen, you recognize when the conversation is no longer productive and politely end the interaction.

Remember, respect is about kindness, understanding, maintaining dignity, and standing up for yourself when necessary. It's not always easy, but it's always worth it.

Respect and Self-Control: Respect is not just about how we treat others, but also about how we control ourselves. It's about maintaining our composure in challenging situations, managing our biases and beliefs, and upholding our character and reputation. It's about demonstrating self-control, even when it's difficult.

Earning Respect: Respect is not an entitlement, it's earned. It's about showing consideration for others' feelings and opinions, acknowledging their rights and choices, and treating them with kindness and understanding. It's about demonstrating through our actions that we are worthy of respect.

Reciprocating Respect: Reciprocating respect is about treating others the way we want to be treated. It's about maintaining a respectful attitude, even when faced with disrespect. It's about rising above personal attacks, remaining calm, and continuing to express our points respectfully.

Walking Away: There are times when the best response is to walk away. When dealing with individuals who refuse to listen or engage in respectful dialogue, it's important to recognize when the conversation is no longer productive and to end the interaction politely. Walking away is not a sign of weakness, but a demonstration of strength and self-respect.

Respect and Dignity: Respect is closely tied to dignity. It's about recognizing the inherent worth of every individual and treating them accordingly. It's about standing up for ourselves and others when this dignity is threatened.

The Value of Respect: Respect is not always easy, but it's always worth it. It fosters understanding, promotes harmony, and builds trust. It's a fundamental aspect of healthy relationships and productive dialogues.

In conclusion, honouring choice is about respecting others' rights to their opinions and decisions, even if we don't agree with them. It's about earning, reciprocating, and demonstrating respect in all our interactions. Remember, respect is not just about how we treat others, but also about how we treat ourselves.

EMBRACING COURAGE

We all have fears, it's part of human nature. Some fears are rational, others are irrational. What's important is not to let these fears control us. Stand up to bullies, face life's challenges, and don't let fear hold you back. Life will present us with many challenges that we may fear, but remember, missed opportunities and regrets often stem from these fears. Embrace courage, overcome your fears, and live in happiness and peace. You are stronger than your fears. You are braver than you believe. And you are capable of more than you can imagine. It is important that you believe in yourself, at times it is hard but when you find yourself in that mindset, reflect back and think about everything which you have went through and how far you came, this will help you relies that your stronger than you actually think. Sometimes it just takes changing your mindset to see your strength or who amazing and good you are, how talented.

Understanding Fear: Fear is a natural human emotion. It's a survival mechanism that alerts us to danger and prepares us to deal with it. However, not all fears are rational or helpful. Some fears are based on past experiences, misconceptions, or irrational thoughts. Understanding the nature of our fears is the first step towards overcoming them.

Facing Fear: Facing our fears is a courageous act. It's about standing up to challenges, confronting our fears head-on, and refusing to let them control us. It's about stepping out of our comfort zone, taking risks, and embracing the unknown.

Overcoming Fear: Overcoming fear is not about eliminating it, but about learning to manage it. It's about developing coping strategies, building resilience, and cultivating a positive mindset. It's about turning our fears into opportunities for growth and self-improvement.

Believing in Yourself: Belief in oneself is a powerful tool in overcoming fear. It's about recognizing our strengths, acknowledging our achievements, and having faith in our abilities. It's about reminding ourselves that we are stronger than our fears, braver than we believe, and capable of more than we can imagine.

Reflecting on Your Journey: Reflecting on our journey can help us realize how far we've come and how much we've grown. It's about acknowledging our struggles, celebrating our victories, and appreciating our progress. It's about recognizing that every challenge we've overcome, every fear we've faced, has made us stronger and more resilient.

Changing Your Mindset: Sometimes, all it takes to see our strength is a change in mindset. It's about shifting our focus from our fears to our capabilities, from our doubts to our achievements. It's about viewing ourselves not as victims of our fears, but as masters of our destiny.

In conclusion, fear is a part of life, but it doesn't have to define us. By understanding our fears, facing them courageously, believing in ourselves, reflecting on our journey, and changing our mindset, we can overcome our fears and live a life of happiness and peace. Remember, you are not defined by your fears, but by your courage to overcome them.

PERSISTENCE PAYS OFF

There's a chance that you won't succeed on the first try, unless you're naturally talented at what you do. When you feel defeated, it's normal for your confidence to be affected and for self-doubt to creep in. But don't let that be your downfall.

In life, you will fall many times, whether in relationships, career, or education. You might feel like you've failed yourself and others who have high expectations of you.

What's most important is how you see yourself. See yourself as someone who tries hard, works hard, gives it their all, and never gives up. See yourself as a human being, not a perfectionist or someone trying to please others' expectations.

Remember, every time you fall, you can rise and try again. If the approach you're using isn't working, then it's time to try a different one.

Reflection Question: Think about a time when you faced a significant challenge or setback. How did you respond? Did you get up and try again, or did it discourage you? How can you apply the lessons from that experience to future challenges? Remember, every setback is an opportunity for a comeback. What steps can you take today to embrace courage and resilience in your life?

These are really important questions to ask yourself, to be able to go through journey of self-reflection and growth, it is important to ask yourself the right questions. With these questions you will get the right insight and you will be able to implement actions for better you.

Persistence: Persistence is about tenacity and endurance. It's about continuing to try, even when faced with challenges or setbacks. It's about not giving up, even when things get tough. Persistence is a key ingredient in the recipe for success.

Resilience: Resilience is the ability to bounce back from adversity. It's about learning from our failures, adapting to change, and continuing to move forward. Resilience is not just about surviving challenges, but thriving in spite of them.

Self-Perception: How we perceive ourselves plays a crucial role in our ability to persist and be resilient. It's important to see ourselves as capable, hardworking individuals who are not defined by our failures or mistakes. We should view ourselves as humans who are constantly learning and growing, not as perfectionists who must meet every expectation.

Adaptability: If one approach isn't working, it's important to be adaptable and willing to try a different one. This could mean changing our strategy, seeking help, or learning new skills. Adaptability is a key component of both persistence and resilience.

Reflection and Growth: Reflecting on our experiences, especially our challenges and setbacks, can lead to significant personal growth. By asking ourselves thoughtful questions, we can gain valuable insights that help us learn from our past and make positive changes for the future.

Taking Action: Finally, it's important to take action. This could mean taking steps to overcome a current challenge, implementing strategies to build resilience, or setting goals for personal growth. Remember, every action, no matter how small, is a step towards a better you.

ACT, DON'T WISH

A lesson is not truly learned unless it is implemented and achieved. It's not enough to merely wish for something; you need to create an action plan and act upon it. Wishing and hoping are part of who we are, part of our biology, but what will yield results are actions, persistence, determination, and commitment. To act and to get the results, you also need to change your ways of thinking and your attitude. A small amount of self-doubt is okay, but if you predominantly think negatively, those are the results you will get.

Action Over Wishing: Wishing for something is the first step towards achieving it. However, wishes alone are not enough. They need to be backed by action. It's about turning our wishes into goals, and our goals into plans. It's about taking concrete steps towards achieving what we desire.

Creating an Action Plan: An action plan is a roadmap that guides us from where we are now to where we want to be. It involves setting clear, achievable goals, identifying the steps needed to achieve these goals, and committing to taking these steps. An action plan gives us direction and helps us stay focused and motivated.

Persistence and Determination: Persistence and determination are key to turning wishes into reality. They involve staying committed to our goals, even in the face of obstacles and setbacks. They involve not giving up, even when things get tough. Persistence and determination are what keep us moving forward, no matter what.

Changing Mindset: Achieving our goals also requires a change in mindset. It's about replacing negative thoughts with positive ones, and self-doubt with self-belief. It's about viewing challenges as opportunities for growth, and failures as stepping stones to success. A positive mindset empowers us to take action and achieve our goals.

Managing Self-Doubt: A certain amount of self-doubt is normal and can even be beneficial, as it keeps us grounded and encourages us to work harder. However, excessive self-doubt can hinder our progress and prevent us from taking action. It's important to manage our self-doubt, to believe in our abilities, and to have faith in our potential. In conclusion, turning wishes into reality is not just about wishing, but about acting, planning, persisting, changing our mindset, and managing our self-doubt. It's about taking control of our lives and shaping our own destiny. Remember, the power to achieve our wishes lies within us. So, let's stop wishing and start doing.

IMPORTANT ANNOUNCEMENT

Hello world, listen carefully. This is an important message to all of you when it comes to your goals or anything that you want to achieve. Wish for it, hope for it, change your thinking, your attitude, believe in yourself. Don't let failure get you down, use it as a learning curve, don't give up, keep fighting and achieve your goals.

Wish for It: Every journey towards achieving a goal begins with a wish, a desire. It's the spark that ignites the fire of ambition within us. It's the first step towards turning our dreams into reality.

Hope for It: Hope is the beacon that guides us through the darkest times. It's the light at the end of the tunnel that keeps us moving forward, even when the odds are against us. Never lose hope, for it is the fuel that powers our journey towards our goals.

Change Your Thinking, Your Attitude: Our thoughts and attitudes shape our reality. A positive mindset can overcome the biggest hurdles, turn failures into lessons, and challenges into opportunities. Cultivate a positive attitude, believe in your abilities, and you'll be amazed at what you can achieve.

Believe in Yourself: Self-belief is the cornerstone of success. It's the unwavering faith in our abilities, the confidence in our potential, and the trust in our journey. Believe in yourself, even when no one else does, and you'll find the strength to overcome any obstacle.

Embrace Failure: Failure is not the opposite of success, but a part of it. It's a stepping stone, a learning opportunity, a chance to grow and improve. Don't let failure get you down. Instead, use it as a learning curve, a chance to grow stronger and wiser.

Don't Give Up, Keep Fighting: The path to achieving our goals is often filled with challenges and setbacks. But remember, the key to success is perseverance. Don't give up, keep fighting, keep moving forward. Every step, no matter how small, brings you closer to your goal.

SELF- LOVE EMBRACE

There are so many different types of love in this world, and all these loves leave a different impact on you, some good and some bad. There are also different types of self-love, but the most important love of them all is self-love. No matter what you go through in life, no matter who you meet, no matter what type of love you experience, always look for that type of love which requires respect. Love yourself enough to be respected by yourself and by others. Self-love and self-acceptance are parts of a worthy journey. This journey requires hard work and commitment. It won't always be easy, and you won't always like what you see. However, it is a journey of healing and self-discovery."

Truth can either destroy you or save you. It's a complex concept. Either way, you might get hurt, but at least you get to do the right thing for yourself and others. It's also important to proceed with caution when speaking the truth as it has to do with the individual. At times, the truth can be difficult to accept. There are people who believe they want to hear the truth, but deep down, they may not be ready for it. What's important is how you approach the subject. Did you know that the truth is actually a complex concept that has been debated by philosophers for centuries? "If you can face your fears and achieve your greatest dreams, the feeling you will get is like being on top of a mountain. Something which was once impossible will become possible."

ACCEPTANCE IS THE KEY

Embrace your flaws, they are part of your growth. Mistakes are stepping stones to learning, not anchors that weigh you down. They shape you, but they are not your identity. Let go of past errors, they only hinder your journey forward. Remember, you are more than your mistakes. Moreover, acceptance is a powerful tool for personal growth. It allows us to move forward from our past mistakes and regrets, which can only cause us pain if we hold onto them. Embracing acceptance leads to self-growth and inner peace, creating a path for us to move forward unburdened. Remember, you are not defined by your past but by the steps you take towards your future."

Acceptance and Self-Growth: Acceptance is a fundamental aspect of self-growth. It's about acknowledging our flaws, mistakes, and passed without judgment. It's about understanding that these are not failures, but lessons that contribute to our personal growth. They are stepping stones that guide us towards becoming better versions of ourselves.

Letting Go of the Past: Holding onto past mistakes and regrets can weigh us down. They can prevent us from moving forward and achieving our full potential. By accepting and letting go of the past, we free ourselves from these burdens. We create space for new experiences, opportunities, and growth.

Embracing Our Flaws: Our flaws are part of who we are. They make us unique. Instead of hiding or denying them, embracing our flaws can lead to self-acceptance and confidence. It's about understanding that nobody is perfect, and that's okay. Our flaws do not define us, but how we handle them does.

Moving Forward: Acceptance allows us to move forward unburdened. It gives us the freedom to make new choices, to take new actions, and to create a new future. It's about focusing on what we can control, and that is our actions and attitudes towards the future.

Defining Our Future: We are not defined by our past, but by the steps we take towards our future. Every step, no matter how small, is progress. It's about making conscious decisions that align with our values and goals. It's about creating a future that reflects who we want to be.

In conclusion, acceptance is not just a key, it's the master key that unlocks self-growth, peace, and a fulfilling future. It's a journey of self-discovery, courage, and transformation. So, embrace acceptance, embrace your journey, and remember, you are more than your past, you are your future.

TIMELESS MOMENTS

Our life is made of small moments we create. These moments could be as simple as a shared laugh with a friend, a quiet moment of solitude in nature, or the joy of achieving a long-sought goal. Each of these moments adds a unique thread to the tapestry of our lives, making it richer and more colorful. So, keep living, keep creating. Cherish these timeless moments, for they are the essence of life."

The Beauty of Simplicity: Often, the most memorable moments in our lives are not grand events, but simple, everyday experiences. A shared laugh with a friend, a quiet moment of solitude in nature, the joy of achieving a goal - these are the moments that truly matter. They may seem insignificant in the grand scheme of things, but they add depth and richness to our lives.

Creating Moments: Life is not just about experiencing moments, but also about creating them. It's about making conscious choices to spend time with loved ones, pursue our passions, and engage in activities that bring us joy. Each moment we create is a reflection of who we are and what we value.

Cherishing Moments: Timeless moments are those that leave a lasting impression on us. They are the moments we cherish and hold close to our hearts. These moments are not defined by their duration, but by the impact they have on us. They are the moments that we remember, that we look back on with fondness, and that shape our lives in meaningful ways.

The Tapestry of Life: Each moment we experience adds a unique thread to the tapestry of our lives. Some threads are vibrant and colourful, representing our happiest moments. Others are dark and dull, representing our challenges and hardships. But together, they create a rich and diverse tapestry that tells our unique story.

The Essence of Life: In the end, life is not measured by the number of breaths we take, but by the moments that take our breath away. These timeless moments, no matter how big or small, are the essence of life. They are the experiences that make life worth living, that bring us joy, and that give us a sense of purpose

INNER CHANGE

Life is a journey with many paths. Each path is unique, shaped by our choices, experiences, and dreams. As you travel your path, remember to create your own memories. These memories are the timeless moments that make your journey uniquely yours. So, follow your own path, embrace your journey, and unlock the potential to create a life filled with meaningful, timeless moments.

Inner Change: Inner change is a transformative process that begins within ourselves. It's about recognizing our potential, embracing our strengths, and addressing our weaknesses. It's about making conscious choices that align with our values, dreams, and aspirations. This inner change not only shapes our journey but also influences the paths we choose to take.

Unique Paths: Each path we take is unique, shaped by our choices, experiences, and dreams. These paths may be filled with challenges and obstacles, but they also bring opportunities for growth, learning, and self-discovery. They are the avenues through which we explore the world, understand ourselves better, and create our own unique journey.

Creating Memories: As we travel our path, we create memories. These memories are the timeless moments that make our journey uniquely ours. They are the snapshots of our experiences, the milestones of our journey, and the markers of our growth. These memories add richness to our journey and serve as reminders of how far we've come.

Embracing the Journey: Embracing our journey is about accepting and appreciating each moment, each experience, and each step we take. It's about celebrating our progress, learning from our setbacks, and remaining open to new experiences. It's about recognizing that our journey is not just about reaching a destination, but about the experiences, growth, and memories we create along the way.

Unlocking Potential: As we embrace our journey and create our own path, we unlock our potential. We discover our strengths, nurture our talents, and realize our dreams. We become the architects of our own life, shaping it with our choices, actions, and experiences.

PAST OR FUTURE

Life presents us with a choice: to remain tethered to the past or to stride towards the future. If you yearn to move forward, the path is clear. Yet, often it's our own fears and doubts that anchor us to bygone times. Ask yourself, what is holding you back? Is it fear of the unknown, or perhaps regret? Remember, the past is a place of reference, not residence. Let go, step forward, and embrace the future. The choice is yours: to be stuck in the past or to look forward to what lies ahead. If you choose to move forward, there is only one way to go.

What's holding you back? Embrace the future with open arms. You are the only one who can make the choice to move on. Where would you love to live the most? Is it in the past or the present, with the benefit of looking towards the future? Are you happy where you are at the moment? These are questions only you can answer for yourself. Do you want to have more regrets? Do you want life to pass you by? And one day, you wake up and realize that you're at the end of your time and you can't redo it again. Doesn't that thought scare you? It's a sobering thought, indeed, and a powerful reminder to live fully in the present, embracing each moment as it comes."

THE POWER OF NOW

The present moment is all we truly have. The past is a collection of moments that have already passed, and the future is but a projection of our hopes and fears. The present, however, is where life happens. It's where we make decisions, experience emotions, and engage with the world around us. It's where we can make a difference.

Yet, how often do we truly live in the present? How often do we let our minds wander to past regrets or future anxieties? How often do we miss the beauty of the present moment because we're too caught up in what was or what might be?

Living in the present means fully engaging with what's happening right now. It means paying attention to the sights, sounds, and sensations around us. It means being mindful of our thoughts and emotions, but not letting them control us. It means making the most of each moment, because each moment is all we really have.

ILLUSION OF CONTROL

One of the reasons we cling to the past or worry about the future is because we crave control. We want to believe that we can shape our lives according to our desires. But the truth is, life is unpredictable. We can't control everything that happens to us. What we can control, however, is how we respond to what happens.

The past is gone, and the future is uncertain. But the present is here, and it's ours to shape. We can choose to dwell on past mistakes or worry about future problems, or we can choose to learn from the past and plan for the future while living fully in the present. The choice is ours.

EMBRACING CHANGE

Change is a fundamental part of life. Everything around us is in a constant state of flux. Yet, we often resist change because it threatens our sense of security. We cling to the familiar, even when it's not serving us well.

But change is not something to be feared. It's something to be embraced. Change is an opportunity for growth. It's a chance to learn, to adapt, and to become stronger. So, instead of resisting change, let's embrace it. Let's see it as an opportunity, not a threat.

THE PARADOX OF TIME

Time is a paradox. It's both infinite and finite. It's always moving, yet it's always still. It's both a healer and a thief. It gives us moments of joy and moments of sorrow. It's a constant reminder of our mortality, yet it also gives us the opportunity to leave a lasting legacy.

The past, present, and future are all interconnected. They're different dimensions of the same reality. The past shapes the present, and the present shapes the future. But the past is not the present, and the present is not the future. They're separate, yet they're one.

THE ART OF LETTING GO

Letting go is an art. It's about releasing the past, embracing the present, and welcoming the future. It's about accepting what was, appreciating what is, and anticipating what could be. It's about finding peace in the midst of chaos, finding hope in the midst of despair, and finding joy in the midst of sorrow.

Letting go is not about forgetting the past, but about learning from it. It's not about ignoring the future, but about preparing for it. It's about living fully in the present, with an open heart and an open mind.

JOURNEY OF LIFE

Life is a journey, not a destination. It's about the experiences we have, the people we meet, and the lessons we learn along the way. It's about the choices we make, the risks we take, and the chances we get to make a difference.

The journey of life is filled with twists and turns, ups and downs, joys and sorrows. But no matter what happens, we must keep moving forward. We must keep striving for better, keep reaching for higher, and keep dreaming of brighter.

CONCLUSION

In the end, the choice between past and future is a false one. The past is a memory, the future is a mystery, but the present is a gift. That's why it's called the present. So, let's unwrap it. Let's make the most of it. Let's live fully in the now, with an eye on the future and a heart that's learned from the past. Because that's the only way to truly live.

WORRY FREE PATH

Cast aside concerns about others' opinions. Your life is your own unique melody, so dance to its rhythm. Embrace the beat and dance freely, unburdened by the world's judgments. Embrace your individuality and let your unique rhythm guide you. Dance to the beat of your own drum, unafraid and unapologetic.

Let go of the fear of judgment and just be yourself. After all, life is a dance floor, and you are the dancer. So, dance like nobody's watching, because your dance is yours alone. It's natural to worry about what others think - it's part of being human. Society can be harsh and judgmental, but it's important not to let that dictate your life. Don't give value to the opinions of others; instead, live your life following your own tune. Your journey is about you and the music you create, not about the spectators on the sidelines.

LOVE STARTS WITH ME

Mirror, mirror on the wall, who do I love most of all? 'I love myself' should always be the answer. You should always love yourself more. The love that you have for yourself is something nobody else can give you. It is a special type of love. Love yourself with pride, honor, respect, and loyalty."

"Self-love is crucial. It's not just about caring for yourself, but also about recognizing the right and healthy way to love and be loved. With self-love, you can foster healthy relationships and interactions, understanding the true essence of love, respect, and care. Self-love is also vital for your overall well-being, contributing to a peaceful and loving life. It allows you to discern how you should be loved and respected. Prioritizing self-love is one of the most important tasks you can undertake. Remember, loving yourself is not a luxury, it's a necessity."

THE JOURNEY TO SELF- LOVE

The journey to self-love is a personal one. It's a path that each of us must walk on our own, yet it's a journey that we all share. It's about learning to accept ourselves as we are, with all our strengths and weaknesses, our successes and failures, our joys and sorrows. It's about learning to love ourselves unconditionally, without judgment or criticism.

THE POWER OF SELF- LOVE

The power of self-love is transformative. It can change the way we see ourselves and the way we interact with the world. It can boost our self-esteem, improve our relationships, and enhance our overall well-being. It can help us to overcome challenges, to persevere in the face of adversity, and to achieve our goals.

THE PRACTICE OF SELF- LOVE

The practice of self-love is a daily commitment. It's about taking care of our physical, emotional, and mental health. It's about setting boundaries and respecting our own needs and desires. It's about celebrating our achievements and learning from our mistakes. It's about being kind to ourselves, forgiving ourselves, and nurturing our inner growth.

THE GIFT OF SELF- LOVE

The gift of self-love is priceless. It's a gift that we give to ourselves, and it's a gift that we can share with others. When we love ourselves, we radiate love and positivity. We attract love and positivity. We inspire love and positivity. And in doing so, we make the world a little bit brighter, a little bit kinder, and a little bit more loving.

CONCLUSION

In conclusion, love truly does start with me. It starts with each and every one of us. And when we love ourselves, we set the foundation for all other forms of love. We become better partners, better friends, better parents, and better people. So, let's make a commitment to love ourselves, not just today, but every day. Because self-love isn't just a practice, it's a way of life

SELF- VALUE

Appreciate yourself, appreciate others, appreciate what you do and how you do it. Appreciate what you go through in life and yet you're still standing, you're still living and achieving your goals. Appreciate others who are there for you in good times and bad. Loyal friends and loyal family members are hard to find. Your time and energy are important. Don't ever waste them on people who don't appreciate it. Learn how to give your time to the right people."

Self-Appreciation: Self-value begins with self-appreciation. It's about recognizing your worth and acknowledging your achievements, no matter how small. It's about celebrating your strengths, learning from your weaknesses, and being proud of who you are and what you've accomplished.

Valuing Others: Just as it's important to appreciate yourself, it's equally important to appreciate others. Recognize the value they bring into your life, be it through their support, their friendship, or their love. Appreciate their presence in your life and the positive impact they have on you.

Appreciating Life's Journey: Life is a journey filled with ups and downs. Appreciate the journey and the lessons it teaches you. Every experience, good or bad, shapes you and helps you grow. Appreciate these experiences for they make you the person you are today.

Time and Energy: Your time and energy are precious resources. Use them wisely. Invest them in activities that bring you joy, in people who value and respect you, and in pursuits that help you grow and achieve your goals.

Choosing the Right People: Not everyone will value your time and energy. Learn to identify these people and distance yourself from them.

Instead, choose to spend your time and energy on people who appreciate you, who support you, and who enrich your life.

CRAFTING HAPPINESS

Happiness becomes you. What is it that keeps you from being happy? Experiencing happiness as often as we'd like is rare. So, when you do experience it, Savor it. Live in the moment and don't let anyone ruin that precious time. Don't chase happiness; it can't be caught. However, it can find you when the time is right. Remember, you're the only one who can create your own happiness.

"Happiness is not a destination, but a journey. It's found in the small moments that often go unnoticed - a kind word, a shared laugh, a warm meal. It's about appreciating what you have, rather than longing for what you don't. So, look around you, embrace the present, and let happiness find its way to you. After all, the key to happiness lies within you.

Understanding Happiness: Happiness is a state of well-being that encompasses living a good life, one with a sense of meaning and deep contentment. It's more than just a pleasant feeling or fleeting moments of joy. It's an overall appreciation of one's life.

Barriers to Happiness: There are many factors that can keep us from experiencing happiness. These can include stress, negative thinking, lack of self-care, not living in alignment with our values, or not pursuing our passions. Identifying these barriers is the first step towards overcoming them.

Savouring Happiness: When happiness comes our way, it's important to Savor it. This means taking the time to appreciate the moment, to fully experience the joy, and to create a memory of it. Savouring enhances our happiness and helps us to prolong its effects.

Living in the Moment: Happiness is often found in the present moment. It's about being fully engaged in whatever we're doing, not dwelling on the past or worrying about the future. Living in the moment allows us to experience happiness more fully.

Creating Happiness: While we can't control all the circumstances of our lives, we can control how we respond to them. This is where we have the power to create our own happiness. It's about choosing positive attitudes, cultivating gratitude, practicing self-care, pursuing our passions, and spending time with loved ones.

The Right People: Surrounding ourselves with positive, supportive people can greatly enhance our happiness. These are the people who lift us up, inspire us, and bring joy into our lives. They are the ones who help us to see the beauty in life, even in difficult times.

CERTAINTY: THE CALM IN KNOWING

Pay attention to those who say 'I love you'. Make sure people in your life confirm it with actions because actions speak louder than words, and words can be spoken without meaning. If you have any questions in your mind, be sure before you act. Unanswered questions and impulsive actions can lead to disastrous results

"If you're not sure, and you have a question mark above your head, don't follow the road. If it is not proven with actions, don't take that road. There is a reason why you have a question mark above your head. If you're unsure and you don't listen to your instinct, you can get lost, get hurt, and have regrets. Make sure that you don't have a question mark above your head, then proceed."

Certainty: Certainty is a state of being free from doubt. In the context of relationships and actions, it refers to the confidence and assurance you feel when you know something is true or when someone's actions align with their words. It's the calm you experience when you know you're on the right path.

Actions Speak Louder Than Words: This old adage holds true in all aspects of life. Words can be empty and devoid of meaning if they're not backed up by actions. It's easy to say 'I love you', but it takes effort and sincerity to show it. Actions are a more accurate measure of someone's feelings and intentions.

Question Everything: If you have doubts or questions, don't ignore them. These are signals that you need more information or clarity. Ask questions, seek answers, and don't act until, you're sure. Impulsive actions can lead to regrettable outcomes.

Trust Your Instincts: Your instincts are your inner compass, guiding you when you're lost. If something doesn't feel right, it probably isn't. Don't ignore that nagging feeling of doubt or discomfort. Instead, pause, reflect, and reassess the situation.

Proceed With Caution: If you're unsure about a decision or a person, don't rush. Take your time to gather more information, reflect on your feelings, and consult with trusted individuals. Once the question mark above your head is replaced with a period, then you can proceed with confidence.

DISCOVER YOUR OWN WAY

It's normal that we all get lost at times and need help finding our way. It's okay to reach out. However, there are special times and situations that require you to find your own way because nobody else can help you with that. "Be your own person, be your own compass, find your own way, trust yourself"

There are times in life when we can get lost and the compass, we have can't help us find a way. At that time, it depends on the situation and how it has affected you. It's important to turn to others for help and support, or if you need peace, and to find what you are missing in life, take a journey towards self-discovery. At times, we need to travel alone to find the missing pieces."

Self-Reliance: Discovering your own way is about cultivating self-reliance. It's about trusting your instincts, making your own decisions, and taking responsibility for your actions. It's about understanding that while others can guide and support you, ultimately, the path you choose to follow is your own.

Self-Discovery: This journey often involves a process of self-discovery. It's about exploring your interests, passions, values, and beliefs. It's about understanding who you are, what you want, and where you want to go. This process can be challenging, but it's also incredibly rewarding.

Courage: Discovering your own way requires courage. It's about stepping out of your comfort zone, facing your fears, and embracing the unknown. It's about having the courage to make mistakes, learn from them, and keep moving forward.

Patience: It's important to remember that this journey is not a race. It takes time to discover your own way. It's about being patient with yourself, celebrating small victories, and understanding that progress is often slow and non-linear.

Resilience: Lastly, discovering your own way is about resilience. It's about bouncing back from setbacks, adapting to change, and persisting in the face of adversity. It's about understanding that obstacles and challenges are part of the journey, not roadblocks.

THE UNFORESEEN JOURNEY

Knowledge is power, and so is imagination. The most important lesson is knowing how to use both. Imagination and knowledge are infinite. They are powerful tools with the potential to heal, help, destroy, or even kill. Therefore, it's crucial to use them responsibly.

Imagination and knowledge can fuel our creativity and passion, leading to fulfillment. They can transport us to other worlds, away from reality. With the right knowledge and the ability to imagine new alternatives, everything becomes possible. So, harness the child within you and explore these endless possibilities."

The Power of Knowledge: Knowledge is not just about acquiring information. It's about understanding, interpreting, and applying that information in meaningful ways. It's about using that knowledge to make informed decisions, solve problems, and contribute positively to the world. Knowledge broadens our horizons, deepens our understanding, and empowers us to make a difference.

The Magic of Imagination: Imagination, on the other hand, is the ability to envision the unseen, to explore the unexplored. It's about dreaming, creating, and innovating. Imagination allows us to transcend the boundaries of reality, to conceive new ideas, and to see the world from different perspectives. It fuels our creativity, sparks our passion, and inspires us to turn our dreams into reality.

The Intersection of Knowledge and Imagination: When knowledge and imagination intersect, magic happens. Knowledge provides the foundation, the facts, the 'what is'. Imagination provides the vision, the possibilities, the 'what could be'. Together, they empower us to create, innovate, and transform the world in ways we never thought possible.

Responsibility: However, with great power comes great responsibility. Knowledge and imagination are powerful tools, but they must be used responsibly. They have the potential to heal and help, but also to harm and destroy. It's up to us to use them wisely, ethically, and for the greater good.

The Journey: The journey of knowledge and imagination is an unforeseen one. It's a journey of discovery, exploration, and transformation. It's about embracing the unknown, taking risks, and learning from our experiences. It's about harnessing the power of knowledge and the magic of imagination to navigate this journey and shape our own destiny.

HURT: PATH TO RESOLUTIONS

When it hurts, it doesn't just cause pain, it changes you as a person. It alters your perception of life and people. Don't dismiss the pain when it comes. Instead, be present in that moment, reflect. The pain is trying to communicate something to you. Pain has a beginning and an end, but you won't be able to resolve it unless you pay attention and find a way.

There is no end to pain until you make a conscious effort to understand and address what you're feeling and experiencing. It can be daunting and uncomfortable to face your inner demons. However, if you don't take this step, you will always carry the pain with you, and your pain will have 'only a beginning and no end.'"

Emotional Intelligence: Pain, whether physical or emotional, is a signal that something is amiss. It demands our attention and urges us to take action. By acknowledging our pain, we are practicing emotional intelligence. This involves recognizing our emotions, understanding what they're telling us, and managing them effectively.

Healing Process: Healing begins when we confront our pain. It's about understanding its source, its impact on our lives, and how we can address it. This process may involve seeking professional help, such as therapy or counselling, or adopting self-care practices like meditation, journaling, or exercise.

Growth and Transformation: Pain can be a catalyst for growth and transformation. It can change our perspective, make us more resilient, and open our eyes to new possibilities. It's through facing our pain that we often discover our strengths and capabilities.

Letting Go: Letting go of our pain doesn't mean forgetting it. It means accepting what happened, learning from it, and moving forward. It's about releasing the hold that pain has on us and making room for peace, happiness, and new experiences.

Self-Compassion: It's important to treat ourselves with compassion and kindness during this process. It's okay to feel pain, to struggle, and to ask for help. Remember, you're human, and it's okay to not be okay sometimes.

In conclusion, pain is not just an end in itself, but a beginning of a new journey towards healing, growth, and self-discovery. It's a journey that requires courage, patience, and self-compassion

GROW, GIVE, SEEK

It's crucial to remember that it's okay to seek help when you're feeling stuck. Whether it's reaching out to a friend, a family member, or a professional, remember that you're not alone. Life is a continuous learning process, and it's okay to ask for guidance along the way. Embrace the journey with an open heart and mind, and remember, every step forward, no matter how small, is progress.

The journey towards true happiness often begins with self-discovery and acceptance. As we navigate through life, akin to the changing seasons, there are instances when we feel 'stuck in the mud'. This could be due to our inability to move past certain obstacles or the fear of failure that prevents us from taking the next step. In such situations, we may choose to remain stagnant.

However, this choice can lead to a cycle of fear and unhappiness. While we may physically progress in life, our minds and hearts may remain bound to the past, burdening us with heavy emotional baggage."

Breaking Free: The first step towards breaking free from this cycle is acknowledging our fears and obstacles. It's about confronting the 'mud' that keeps us stuck. This could be a past failure, a fear of rejection, or even a lack of self-belief. Acknowledging these barriers is not a sign of weakness, but a testament to our courage and the first step towards overcoming them.

Self-Acceptance: Self-acceptance is a powerful tool in this journey. It's about accepting ourselves for who we are, with all our strengths and weaknesses. It's about understanding that it's okay to be imperfect, to make mistakes, and to have flaws. Self-acceptance frees us from the burden of trying to be someone we're not and allows us to embrace our true selves.

Growth Mindset: Adopting a growth mindset can also help us move past our obstacles. A growth mindset is the belief that our abilities and intelligence can be developed through dedication and hard work. It's about viewing challenges as opportunities for growth, and failures as stepping stones towards success.

Support and Guidance: As you mentioned, seeking help is a crucial part of this journey. It's about understanding that we don't have to face our challenges alone. There are people around us - friends, family, mentors, or professionals - who can provide support, guidance, and a fresh perspective.

Moving Forward: Finally, it's about taking that next step, no matter how small. Every step forward is progress, and every effort counts. It's about celebrating our small victories and using them as motivation to keep going.

In conclusion, the journey towards true happiness is not about avoiding the 'mud', but learning how to navigate through it. It's about self-discovery, self-acceptance, growth, and moving forward. And remember, you're not alone in this journey. Reach out, seek help, and keep going. Every step you take brings you closer to your destination.

MISTAKES LESSONS

When you encounter a harsh lesson, irrespective of whether it's self-inflicted or imposed by others, avoid repeating it and prevent others from inflicting the same upon you. Absorb its teachings, so you won't have to endure a similar situation in the future. A lesson truly absorbed is a mistake not repeated."

Forbid yourself from making the same mistake twice. Do your best not to follow the same route. Remind yourself, how did you feel after you did something that hurt you and others? What did you feel? What did others feel? How did your life and the lives of others change?" do your best not to be to hard on yourself, I understand that at times we are really harsh on ourselves, it is important to learn that you do the best that you can and at times what counts the most, is actually how you feel about what has occurred and if you have learned a lesson.

SELF- REFLECTION EMPOWERMENT

When uncertainty clouds your judgment, take a moment to reflect. Your doubts are not unfounded. Hasty decisions and an unsettled mind can lead to undesirable outcomes and regrets. Avoid impulsive actions.

Just as the tree sees its own reflection in the water, we too can gain insights by looking inward. This introspection, coupled with acquired knowledge, can be a powerful tool for personal growth and empowerment.

Moreover, our self-reflection can manifest in our behavior and interactions with others and ourselves. It influences how we perceive ourselves. Just like the tree is visible in its reflection, we can see the effects of our self-reflection in our actions and attitudes. This process of self-reflection, therefore, is not just about understanding ourselves better, but also about improving our interactions with the world around us.

Self-Empowerment: Self-reflection is a powerful tool for self-empowerment. It allows us to take control of our lives, make informed decisions, and become proactive rather than reactive. It empowers us to take responsibility for our actions and their consequences, and to make changes where necessary.

Growth: Self-reflection is an essential part of personal growth. It allows us to learn from our mistakes, understand our strengths and weaknesses, and continuously strive for improvement. It's through reflecting on our actions and experiences that we gain insights and wisdom.

Mindfulness: Self-reflection promotes mindfulness. It encourages us to live in the present moment, to be aware of our thoughts, feelings, and actions, and to understand how they impact our well-being and the world around us.

Empathy: By understanding ourselves better through self-reflection, we can also develop empathy for others. We can understand their perspectives, feelings, and experiences, which can improve our relationships and interactions.

Self-Awareness: Self-reflection enhances self-awareness. It helps us understand our values, beliefs, and motivations. This self-awareness is crucial in making decisions that align with our authentic selves and in leading a fulfilling life.

BABY STEPS, DARLING

Take small steps; these will lead you to big ones. Take it one step at a time. To create big steps and to reach your goal or destination, you need to follow the right steps.

Patience is the key when it comes to achieving your goals. It doesn't matter what those goals are, whether emotional or practical; there are rules for following the right steps. The goals must be realistic, desired, and prioritized.

It is important to stay committed. It is important to know that it won't be easy. You will need to be willing to fight every obstacle. It is important to be prepared in case you don't achieve your goal when you wish to. At times, we are not able to achieve our goals when we desire, but when the timing is right.

Adaptability: In the journey towards your goals, it's crucial to be adaptable. The path may not always be straight or predictable. There may be detours, roadblocks, and unexpected turns. Being adaptable means being open to change, ready to adjust your strategies, and willing to learn from each experience.

Resilience: Resilience is the ability to bounce back from setbacks and keep going in the face of adversity. It's about having a positive mindset and viewing failures not as the end, but as learning opportunities. Remember, every successful person has faced and overcome numerous challenges.

Consistency: Consistency is key in achieving your goals. It's about taking small, consistent actions every day that bring you closer to your goal. It's not about making huge leaps, but about making steady progress over time.

Support System: Don't underestimate the power of a strong support system. Surround yourself with positive, like-minded individuals who encourage and inspire you. They can provide valuable advice, motivation, and even constructive criticism that can help you stay on track.

Self-Care: Lastly, don't forget to take care of yourself. Achieving your goals is important, but so is maintaining your health and well-being. Make sure to take time for rest, relaxation, and activities that you enjoy. This will help you stay energized and motivated on your journey.

MOVING BEYOND THE PAST

The root of all your suffering is attachment to whatever or whoever has hurt you. Let it go. You have carried it long enough. It is time to give yourself a break. You did your part, let it go and look forward. Breathe easy.

Set yourself free from the burdens of your past, from the burdens of your current state. Set yourself free and fly. There is no need to carry with you what you already went through. Don't let it weigh you down. Don't allow it to create imbalance in your life. Let yourself rest. Let your back and shoulders rest." Embrace the present moment, for it is a gift. It's the only place where life exists. Let the winds of change lift you higher, let them carry you towards new beginnings and opportunities. Remember, every sunrise offers a chance to start anew, to rebuild and reshape your life the way you want it to be. You are not defined by your past, but by the choices you make in the present. So, choose wisely, choose happiness, choose freedom. **Move beyond the past, and look into the future."**

PERCEPTIONS & INTERPRETATIONS

It is hard to feel okay, or to move on when your point did not get across the bridge, or when someone interprets it in a different way. It causes a lot of conflicts and anxiety. What's important is that you do your part, say it as clearly as possible, believe in what you say, stand behind it, and just move on. You can't change how others either think or feel about you, and even how they interpret what you say. Save yourself a lot of trouble by not fighting or repeating your point.

People will only hear what they want to hear, so why waste your breath explaining? Everybody hears what they want to hear. Say your piece and let them believe what they want. All you need to know is that you did your part, you were honest, you know the truth. There's no need to do anything else, because at the end of the day, people believe and hear what they want to hear. So, hear me say this, it is ok.

DEEDS NOT WORDS

You can hope for it, you can wish for it, you can dream about it, but if you don't actually do anything about it, it will never become a reality. It will always remain a wish, a missed goal, a missed dream. Remember, the journey towards achieving your dreams begins with a single step. Don't just stand on the sidelines of your life, watching your dreams pass you by. Step into the arena, take that first step, and start turning your dreams into reality. It's never too late to start, and every moment wasted is a moment you won't get back. So, seize the day, take action, and watch as your dreams unfold into reality."

You can implement this into every aspect of your life, it is not just for your goals, dreams, it can be utilized in friendships, and romantic relationships, family, work

SEIZE THE MOMENT

Stop trying to understand life. You can't, and you won't be able to, because life is there to be lived, not understood. Live your life to the fullest. We all want to understand life, or why things happened the way they did. But unfortunately, we can't understand everything. Some things are not meant to be understood, like life itself. Life is meant to be lived. Keep living, keep having fun as long as you can.

I DARE YOU

Step out of your comfort zone and dare to be wild. Let go of the fear of the unknown, the fear of failure, the fear of judgment. Be spontaneous, embrace the unpredictability of life. Try something new, something that excites you, something that scares you. Challenge yourself, push your limits, test your boundaries. You will learn and grow in the most challenging and beautiful ways. You'll discover strengths you never knew you had; passions you never knew existed. Dare to live, dare to explore, dare to be wild."

Dare to dream. Dare to envision a future that fills your heart with joy and your mind with wonder. Dare to imagine a life that isn't limited by the boundaries of what's familiar or safe. Dare to be different. Embrace your uniqueness, your individuality. Don't be afraid to stand out, to go against the grain, to choose a path that's uniquely yours. And most importantly, dare to be you. Authentic, unapologetic, beautifully you."

LIVING LIFE FULLY

Remember, a meaningful life is a journey, not a destination. It's about who you become in the process of pursuing your goals and dreams. It's about being true to yourself, standing up for what you believe in, and making a difference in the world in your own unique way.

So, ask yourself: What kind of life do you want to live? What kind of person do you want to be? What kind of impact do you want to have on the world? The answers to these questions will guide you towards a life of purpose and meaning. So, dare to dream, dare to believe, and most importantly, dare to live.

What is your definition of a meaningful life? When you know it, you will live it, but only if you're ready for it. Every type of life requires hard work and sacrifice. What are you prepared to lose to gain what you want? To live the life, you want with purpose and with meaning.

A meaningful life is not just about pursuing happiness, but also about connecting with others, contributing to the world, and living in alignment with your values. It's about finding your passion and pursuing it relentlessly. It's about learning and growing, embracing challenges, and turning obstacles into opportunities.

A STORM TO WEATHER

Life and its lessons can be as fierce as a storm, capable of altering us, even breaking us. Yet, it's in these moments that we find the strength to rebuild ourselves. With hard work, anything is possible. All we need to do is brave the storm.

Remember, storms don't last forever. They leave behind clear skies and a chance for a fresh start. So, let's embrace the storm, learn from it, and emerge stronger.

Life experiences can be as harsh as stormy weather, leaving indelible marks on our souls. The most valuable lessons are those we've lived through and learned from. If we fail to learn, these lessons merely scar us, and we carry them forward with unchanged perceptions. Without understanding, lessons lose their meaning.

EMBRACING OPPORTUNITIES

Make step towards a new career or relationship, or we want to let go of the past but we fear that we might not be able to do that. Whatever you wish, or need, or want to let go of. You won't know unless you challenge yourself and get to the other side of the bridge. Remember, every step you take towards overcoming your fears brings you one step closer to your goals. **Keep going.**

If you don't cross the bridge, how will you know what is waiting for you on the other side? Great possibilities might await you. **Don't allow irrational fear to control you and take away the best opportunities from you.**

Reach out for a better life, reach out for passion, reach out for happiness, reach out for a better you.

There are times, moments in our lives where we are either at the beginning of something new, or in the middle of something new, and we are just afraid to cross that bridge because we don't know what is waiting for us on the other side.

BE YOUR OWN SUPERHERO

A person can't hurt you unless you give them the power and weapons to do so. Be careful who you trust; sometimes even your friend can be your enemy. In life, you will meet many different people. Some will change you for the better, some for the worse. You will get hurt, and pain will challenge you in more ways than one, because, that's what pain does. Just remember that you're stronger than you think. Believe in your own strength."

"Work hard to be your own best friend, to be your own hero. People who might help you or who have been there for you won't always be able to stand by your side. Learn how to be your own hero. Embrace the journey of self-discovery and self-improvement. Understand that every experience, good or bad, shapes you and adds to your strength.

Remember, being your own hero isn't just about overcoming external challenges, but also about conquering your inner fears and doubts. It's about standing tall even when you're standing alone, and knowing that you have the power within you to rise above any situation.

EMBRACE UNKNOWN: YOUR STORY

Fear Holds You Back. Don't fear starting over. This time, it can be completely different. The choices you made in the past won't dictate your present and won't affect your future. Change the way you used to make choices. Embrace the uncertainty of the new. Let the thrill of the unknown guide you. Remember, every moment is a fresh beginning. It's never too late to rewrite your story.

THE POWER IS IN SELF- BELIEF

Believe in yourself. This belief will be your driving force for success. Belief is a powerful tool that will help you move forward and achieve your goals. It's the foundation upon which you build your dreams. It gives you the courage to face challenges, the confidence to take risks, and the resilience to keep going even when things get tough.

If you believe in yourself, you will go far in life. If you focus on your goal, you will also go far. And if you don't let the opinions of others influence you, you will reach even further."

Remember, every step you take in the direction of your dreams is a step towards becoming your own superhero. Keep believing, keep focusing, and keep going!

TAKE CHARGE

You're the only one who is holding yourself back. We are often our own biggest obstacles, and overcoming our self-imposed limitations is a crucial step towards personal growth and happiness. If you want something, you are the only one who can get it. You will need to fight through all of the obstacles. You will need to stay committed, determined, and strong, because it won't be easy but it will be worth it in the end.

PUT THE PIECES TOGETHER

Pain and life change you. Over time, you may lose small pieces of yourself. Sometimes, these pieces may be damaged or even completely broken. You will change, but you will also be able to put yourself back together. With time, self-love, determination, and healing, you won't be the same, just like a tree. But you will be different, stronger, and more beautiful, with your own unique story.

Life will make you grow, just like a tree. Be aware that over time, as seasons pass, you may lose leaves, which represent pieces of yourself, and you will experience changes. When that happens, breathe in and out, calm yourself down, think things through, learn, make peace, and move on. This is how you put the pieces back. Your journey is a testament to the transformative power of resilience and personal growth."

LIVE IN A PRESENT

Live in the Present "Yesterday happened, today is here, tomorrow will come. Focus on the here and now. You can't get it back, so don't waste these moments. We tend to focus on the future and the past, and by doing so, we don't live in the here and now. We miss amazing opportunities, memories that we could have created, and lessons that we could have learned."

LOTUS - NELUMBO NUCIFER

The lotus flower symbolizes purity, rebirth, spirituality, and endurance. Every religion has a different perception and belief about this beautiful flower. We are like a beautiful lotus flower; we rise from the dark and bloom in a beautiful way. With every life experience, we grow in different directions. When we are stuck in the dark, we rise beautifully when the time is right, even if it is with struggle. But we do emerge as even more beautiful creations of God, just like the lotus."

ACTION OVER HOPE

What's important is to make sure we understand what we wish for or hope for. When we are hurt by someone or when someone has made us angry, we can say so many things in the heat of the moment, not knowing that life is so tricky and that one day it can come true. So, be careful what you wish for; you will never know if you can handle it unless it has projected itself in front of you.

Moreover, it's essential to remember that our wishes and hopes are just the beginning. They set the direction, but it's our actions that move us forward. It's not enough to simply wish or hope for something; we must also take the necessary steps to make it happen. Life is a journey, and while our wishes and hopes can guide us, it's our actions that define our path."

THE UNSEEN GUARDIAN

Focus it is important. If something doesn't feel right, listen to your gut instinct. It is telling you something that you can't hear or see. Trust your gut. A gut feeling, or intuition, is a thought that pops into your mind when something doesn't feel right. Pay attention, listen, and follow it. A gut feeling is a survival signal. It is there to keep us safe and alive. It's known to relate to fearful and reactive behavior. When we experience that type of behavior, even before we fully experience danger, our intuition sends us warning signals.

Moreover, it's worth noting that our intuition is honed from our past experiences and knowledge. It's our subconscious mind drawing on our past experiences and knowledge to protect us. It's a powerful tool that can guide us in decision-making and problem-solving. However, while our intuition can be incredibly insightful, it's also important to balance it with rational thinking. Our intuition might alert us to potential dangers, but rational thinking allows us to evaluate the situation objectively and decide on the best course of action.

Remember, trusting your intuition doesn't mean ignoring logic or facts. It's about listening to and honoring your instincts, but also critically evaluating the situation. Your intuition and rational mind are two sides of the same coin, and they work best when used together.

YOU'RE AMAZING

Do the best that you can do, for yourself and others. That's all that anyone can ask for. Don't stress if things don't work out or if you don't achieve the desired outcome immediately. Things will fall into place when they're supposed to. The most important part is that you keep trying. That's what truly counts in the end. Remember, every effort you make, no matter how small, is a step forward. Celebrate your progress, learn from your setbacks, and never stop believing in yourself. You're doing amazing, and it's important to acknowledge that."

GROWTH IN TRYING

You will always be a winner, even when you lose. It's all about how you perceive failure. See it as an opportunity to grow and learn. Of course, we all want to win, whether in our careers, school competitions, or in the world. But there's something more special when it comes to winning. It's actually about understanding that winning is not everything. It's not about how you win or if you win, it's about the fact that you tried and you learned about yourself. It's about not having regrets because you didn't do this or try that out of fear that you would lose and others would laugh at you. It's about trying, enjoying the process, and finding peace afterwards."

YOUR BREAKTHROUGHS

Don't forget to celebrate when you achieve your goals. Don't forget to learn and understand what you're thinking and feeling. Don't forget that you can do it. Don't forget not to be hard on yourself. Don't forget to love yourself. Don't forget to say, 'I am worthy of love and respect. We always spend so much time hating, hurting, and investing in that, letting it sink into our hearts, minds, and lives. We give it so much time, but when it comes to good things in our lives and our achievements, we barely give it a clap. Invest in celebrating instead. Just have fun and enjoy, and capture those memories. You will need it one day when you're hurting, to show you that feeling good is possible in this life, and it will happen again. When you're in your golden years, these memories will keep you company.

In addition, remember that every step you take towards healing and happiness is a victory. Celebrate your progress, no matter how small it may seem. Each moment of joy, each instance of progress, each act of kindness to yourself is a testament to your strength and resilience. You are not defined by your pain, but by your courage to persist and thrive despite it. So, keep going, keep growing, and keep celebrating the wonderful person you are.

RESILIENCE: SURVIVOR

When your world is turned upside down, when your heart is bleeding, when your feet are hurting, when you feel like you don't fit in with the rest of them, know your own pain, know your own strength. Don't allow your struggles to be mocked, don't desire to be like everybody else. You're you, and you're great just the way you are. Be proud of what you've achieved, how you've survived, how you've dealt with everything you went through. It wasn't easy, and you probably regret many things, including different ways you have dealt with it, but at least you fought, and survived. You're still standing, and that takes courage, to fight when you have no strength anymore.

Take time for yourself, learn how to heal, as healing is a life journey, especially when you experience traumas. It takes time, so take time to just breathe and enjoy what makes you happy, what gives you peace. Learn about your triggers and how you can manage them to prevent the stress, anxiety, intrusive thoughts, anger, and pain from recurring with the same strength as it occurred when you first experienced what caused you such distress. People might judge you and call you names, but with everything you've been through, that shouldn't bother you anymore.

THE PRICE OF EVERY ACTION

Life doesn't offer free lessons; every choice we make comes with a price. Each decision we make, each action we take, is like a transaction in the bank of life. We pay with our time, our energy, our emotions, and sometimes, our well-being. Making a choice is like tossing a coin. You never know

which side you'll get unless you decide to toss that coin. Every single time you toss the coin, you may receive a different side, sometimes the same. It's a gamble. But unlike a coin toss, the outcomes of our choices are not left to chance. They are shaped by our actions, our attitudes, and our determination to succeed.

So, be mindful of the choices you make and how you proceed from there. Understand that every choice, no matter how small, can have a profound impact on your life. It can set you on a path towards success or lead you astray. But remember, even if you make a wrong turn, you always have the power to correct your course. You have the power to learn, to grow, and to make better choices in the future.

THE BEAUTY OF BEING YOU

Each one of us is unique in our own way. This uniqueness is not just about the differences in our appearances or ways of thinking, but it's also about the distinct perspectives we bring, the diverse experiences we have, and the varied skills we possess. This uniqueness adds value to the world and makes it a more interesting place.

When you are true to yourself, you can make a significant impact on the world in your own unique way. This could be through your profession, your passion, or simply by being a good human being. The way you touch people's lives, bring about positive changes, and contribute to society is truly beautiful.

Being different is not just okay, it's beautiful. It's a testament to the diversity of life. So, be proud of who you are, celebrate your uniqueness, and remember, the world needs you just as you are

CONTINUAL GROWTH

You will always be a work in progress, and that's a beautiful thing. It means you're continually evolving, learning, and growing. There's always room for improvement because perfection is not a destination, it's a journey.

Work on yourself, keep improving, keep growing, and keep developing towards a better you. Remember, every step you take, no matter how small, is progress. Every book you read, every new skill you learn, every mistake you make, and every challenge you overcome is part of your growth.

Don't be discouraged by the pace of your progress. Instead, celebrate each milestone, no matter how small. Keep pushing, keep striving, and keep evolving. After all, the only person you should try to be better than is the person you were yesterday

LESSONS, NOT THE BAGGAGE

Every day is a new day. You're the one who can decide how you're going to spend it, either dwelling on what happened previously or moving on and living. Sort out what you went through, take time for yourself, heal, learn, let it go, let it be, and move on with your life.

You have experienced hardship in your past. Your past experiences have shaped you, influenced your growth, and made you the person you are today. The important part is that you let it go. Allowing your past experiences to overshadow your present may prevent you from fully experiencing and enjoying the present moment. It's essential to remember that while our past shapes us, it does not define us.

Our ability to learn and grow from our experiences is one of our greatest strengths as humans. Use the lessons learned to improve your life, to educate others when needed, and to live without carrying the burden of the past on your shoulders. Remember, every new day brings with it new opportunities for growth and self-improvement. Embrace these opportunities and continue on your journey towards becoming the best version of yourself.

PLAY, FORWARD, REWIND

Focus on what you can control. Why waste life's precious moments and energy into something which is beyond your control?

There are so many things in life which are beyond our control, such as the weather, the passage of time, or the actions of others. However, there are also aspects of our life and world that are within our control, like our reactions, our attitudes, and our actions. There is a balance between these two, but it is important to give your energy and focus to things which you can control and change.

Understanding this balance is key to living a fulfilling life. When we focus on what we can control, we empower ourselves. We can make decisions that align with our values and goals. We can take actions that bring us closer to our aspirations. We can choose to react positively to challenges and setbacks, viewing them as opportunities for growth rather than obstacles.

On the other hand, when we expend energy worrying about things beyond our control, it can lead to stress, frustration, and a feeling of helplessness.

By letting go of what we can't control, we free up mental and emotional space to invest in areas where we can make a real difference.

So, embrace the power you have over your own life. Use it to shape your journey in a way that reflects who you are and who you want to be. Remember, the most significant changes often come from the smallest steps taken in the right direction.

SPREAD POSITIVITY

"The way we can destroy our world together, we can also work by changing that and working together in peace to protect our earth, our loved ones. It takes one positive thought, one positive word, a kind smile, a helping hand.

Just as our actions have the power to harm, they also have the power to heal and protect. It's about making conscious choices every day. Choosing to recycle instead of waste, to speak words of kindness instead of anger, to lend a hand instead of turning a blind eye.

These small acts, when multiplied by millions of people, can transform the world. Remember, every positive action counts, and together, we can make a significant difference.

In this journey, it's important to remember that change starts with us. As individuals, we have the power to influence those around us through our actions and attitudes. So, let's choose positivity, kindness, and sustainability. Let's be the change we wish to see in the world."

THE 'YES' DOOR

When one door closes, another opens. Focus on what lies ahead, not on the closed door. There's no going back, so don't waste time. The open door can close over time, and you might miss what was waiting for you. Life will close many doors, but it will also open them. Patience is key. Realize that closed doors can't be unlocked. Process your experiences and feelings, and make peace with them. It's important not to give up. Clarity and an open mind are crucial, as is the desire to open another door. If you're held back by focusing on the doors you can't open, you'll miss your opportunities when the right doors open.

Every door in life, whether open or closed, represents an experience. Open doors are opportunities waiting to be seized, while closed doors symbolize lessons learned and chapters ended. It's crucial to remember that every closed door has shaped you into who you are today, and every open door presents a chance for growth and new experiences. Embrace the journey of life with its ups and downs, knowing that each door leads you closer to your true self and your purpose. Remember, the 'Yes' Door is not just an opportunity, but a testament to your resilience and optimism. Keep moving forward, and the right doors will open at the right time.

I PUNCH HARDER

Life throws many punches. After the first punch, learn to dodge them. A hit once is okay, but twice in the same place shows a lack of learning or attention. Learn how and when to dodge, and pay attention. If you make a mistake in life, learn not to repeat it. As long as you're standing, fight with everything you have. Decide the role you want to play in life. Life is like a boxing ring. It's not about the punches you throw, but about the punches you can take and still keep moving forward. It's about resilience, about bouncing back stronger after every hit. It's about learning from each punch, each mistake, and using that knowledge to dodge future blows. It's about standing tall, no matter how hard life hits. Remember, every champion was once a contender who refused to give up. So, keep fighting, keep learning, and keep standing up. After all, the greatest victory is not in never falling, but in rising every time we fall.

Quote: "You don't lose if you get knocked down, you lose if you stay down." - Muhammad Ali

PURPOSEFUL WALK: YOUR MARK

You can walk a hundred miles, but if you don't have the vision and direction to where you are going, then what is the point of walking? In life, you will take many different roads. Some will lead to greatness and some will lead you to hardships. Make sure that you have good shoes on; those will take you a long way.

Life is a journey, not a destination. It's about the steps you take, the paths you choose, and the marks you leave behind. It's about the courage to step into the unknown, the strength to endure hardships, and the wisdom to learn from every experience. It's about leaving a legacy that inspires future generations. So, walk with purpose, act with conviction, and let your journey be your legacy.

Quote: "Walk and do, leave your mark on this world, leave your legacy let future people know that you were here."

PEACE: HAPPINESS KEY

Every problem in life has a solution, even when it seems impossible. When you feel trapped, remember that circumstances can change. As long as you're alive, there's hope. The only certainty is death, the one thing that can't be changed.

Life presents us with various challenges, coming at us from all directions. Sometimes, it may seem like there are no solutions. However, this often depends on your mindset and determination at that time. Most problems have solutions, but they may not be immediate. Solutions often don't arrive on our preferred schedule.

Just as there are many problems, there are also many approaches to solving them, much like in mathematics. The key is to maintain peace of mind, knowing that every problem has a solution, and that solution will come in its own time.

Embrace the journey of life with its ebbs and flows. Remember, it's not the destination, but the journey that shapes us. Each challenge is a stepping stone to growth. Each victory, a testament to our resilience. So, keep moving forward with peace in your heart and a clear vision in your mind. After all, happiness isn't just about the absence of problems, but the ability to deal with them.

SACRIFICE & COMPROMISE

Sacrifices are never easy. Despite this, everyone has desires they yearn to fulfill. To gain what your heart truly desires, you must be willing to compromise and make sacrifices. Life is filled with contrasts - good and bad, dark and light. It's also filled with various elements that require our attention - work, family, friends, and personal goals. Learning to manage and balance all of these aspects is crucial. It's about learning to compromise and make sacrifices to achieve the right balance, leading to happiness and less stress.

Indeed, the art of balance is a continuous journey It's about understanding that not all things can be achieved at once. Prioritizing what's important to you at a given moment is key. Sometimes, this might mean putting your personal goals on hold to focus on family or work. Other times, it might mean taking a step back from your busy schedule to invest time in self-care and personal growth. Remember, it's okay to say no to

things in order to maintain your balance.

It's not about having it all, but about having what truly matters to you. And most importantly, it's about being at peace with your decisions, knowing they are leading you towards your desired life. This is the true essence of learning to balance through sacrifice and compromise.

GROWTH AND DISCOVERY

You won't learn anything unless you go out and put yourself out there. Your life lessons are waiting for you in the world. Fear not, go live, go experience, and discover who you are. Live, explore, learn, experience, have fun. You only live once, create amazing memories.

Absolutely, stepping out of your comfort zone is the first step towards growth. Embrace the unknown and let it shape you. The world is a vast canvas, waiting for you to paint your story. Each experience, each interaction, is a brushstroke that adds color and depth to your life's masterpiece.

The 'green' signifies growth, renewal, and life. It's a call to action - to embrace life in all its glory. It's about saying yes to new experiences, yes to challenges, and yes to life itself. It's about making the most of the time you have, for you only live once. So, go ahead, paint your canvas green. Let each moment be a vibrant splash of joy, learning, and memories. Remember, life isn't about the destination, it's about the journey. So, GO GREEN, live fully, and enjoy the ride.

YOU ARE NO. 1

Prioritize your health, without your health the goals, dreams, peace, and happiness does not exist because health is vital for life, everything else flows. You are the only one who can decide if you will be okay, if you will let the past go, if you will focus on taking care of yourself, and putting yourself first, if you will be happy.

You're the one with the power, change what you can, don't allow yourself to be held down by painful life experiences, by negative people, by people's opinions. If you want to be Okay, you will make it happen, be strong enough to want that, be strong enough to make it happen. Remember, prioritizing your health is not a selfish act. It's about understanding that you need to be in your best shape to be able to give your best to the world. So, take that step today, put yourself first, and watch as everything else falls into place. You have the power to create the life you desire. So, make your health your number one priority, and embrace the journey towards a happier, healthier you. You are your number one priority.

WISDOM OF THE AGES

Listen to your elders. These are the individuals who have lived longer than you and have gained lifelong lessons through hardships and shattered dreams. Learn from someone who has already traversed the path you are about to embark on.

Elders carry with them a wealth of knowledge and wisdom, shaped by the myriad experiences they've had. Their advice is often a reflection of the lessons they've learned, the mistakes they've made, and the successes they've achieved. They can provide guidance, helping you navigate your own journey with a deeper understanding and foresight. Remember, every person's journey is unique, and while you carve your own path, the wisdom of elders can serve as a guiding light. It can help you avoid certain pitfalls and make informed decisions. So, listen attentively, absorb their wisdom, and apply it in your own life. Their experiences are not just stories, but valuable lessons that can enrich your life journey."

EMBRACING THE PRESENT

Don't fret over what you can't have, instead, focus on what you could lose and ensure you protect that. Worrying about the unattainable can often blind us to the treasures we already possess. Worrying is a part of all of us, but what's truly important is discerning if it's worth the worry. Take a moment to sit back and relax. Breathe in the fresh air, feel the breeze on your face, bask in the warmth on your skin. Immerse yourself in these sensations and focus on how they make you feel. This is the essence of mindful living - being present in the moment and appreciating the simple joys of life.

Remember, life is a series of moments. Don't let worries of the past or anxieties of the future steal your present. Embrace the now, for it's all we truly have. Let this awareness guide you towards a life of contentment and peace. After all, the beauty of life lies in the journey, not the destination

SELF- LOVE AND APPRICIATION

Take a moment to say, 'Thank you' to yourself. You have done well under the circumstances. It's important to learn not to be too hard on yourself. You've achieved so much, even in times when it felt like there was no energy left inside you to fight. You need to appreciate everything you've accomplished, not just for yourself, but also for others.

I'm sure it wasn't easy, dealing with differing opinions and personalities. At times, we have to compromise and put others' needs above our own. Some situations don't allow us to prioritize ourselves. However, remember that every act of kindness you've extended, every compromise you've made, has made a difference. It's these selfless acts that truly define us and our journey. So, take pride in your journey, for it is uniquely yours and no one else's.

We are programmed by biology, nature, and psychology to be hard on ourselves, to be negative. **This is called negative bias in Psychology.** But think about it - if you can put so much energy into beating yourself up for mistakes, regrets, missed opportunities, and more, you can also learn to love yourself, appreciate what you do for others, and what you achieve and go through in life, and how you survive it. If you can be negative, you can learn how to be positive as well.

Remember, every step you take, every decision you make, is shaping your journey. So, be kind to yourself, appreciate your efforts, and embrace the power of positivity. After all, the most important relationship you have is with yourself.

Another important aspect of self-reflection involves learning from others. This is where the life lessons of famous individuals come into play. These lessons can be beneficial to us all, as they provide practical examples of how to navigate life's challenges and opportunities. They teach us the importance of being open-minded, not judging others, and seeing things from different perspectives. This can help us learn from others and apply these lessons in our own lives.

In addition to learning from the experiences of famous individuals, we can also learn from the people we interact with daily. Our family, friends, colleagues, and even strangers can offer valuable insights. Each person we meet has a unique life story filled with lessons that can enrich our understanding of the world.

For instance, a friend's resilience in the face of adversity can inspire us to be more persistent in pursuing our goals. A colleague's innovative problem-solving approach can encourage us to think outside the box. Even a brief interaction with a stranger can teach us about kindness, empathy, or the beauty of diversity.

Moreover, learning from others isn't limited to their successes. Understanding their mistakes and failures can be equally enlightening. It allows us to avoid similar pitfalls and accelerates our personal growth and development.

Therefore, as we journey through life, let's remember to keep our minds open, listen attentively, and be willing to learn from everyone we meet. This practice of continuous learning from others complements our self-reflection process and empowers us to lead richer, more fulfilling lives.

Cultural Exchange: Interacting with people from diverse cultural backgrounds can broaden our perspectives and foster a deeper understanding of different cultures. This can enhance our empathy and tolerance, and enrich our own cultural identity.

Skill Acquisition: We can learn new skills and improve existing ones by observing and interacting with others. For example, a family member's cooking technique, a friend's musical talent, or a colleague's presentation skills can inspire us to learn and grow.

Emotional Intelligence: By observing how others handle their emotions, we can learn to manage our own emotions better. This can lead to improved relationships and better decision-making.

Conflict Resolution: Observing how others handle conflicts can provide valuable lessons on negotiation, compromise, and problem-solving.

Resilience: Life stories of people overcoming challenges can teach us resilience and the ability to bounce back from adversity.

THE POWER OF SELF-REFLECTION

Self-reflection is a powerful tool that helps you develop your skills and review their effectiveness. Rather than merely experiencing life's moments and continuing without pause, it's essential to ask questions. Seeking answers and understanding oneself is a vital part of life. While some people may go through life without self-reflection, adding varying degrees of value to their experiences, others recognize the importance of introspection.

Self-reflection is about questioning. It's about gaining insight into your thought processes, emotional intelligence, and behavior. It's about understanding, figuring out, learning, growing, and making different choices—choices that will benefit you in the long run.

Remember, every question you ask yourself opens a door to self-discovery. Every answer you find is a step towards self-improvement. Take the time to get to know yourself. Embrace the journey of self-reflection, for it leads to the most rewarding destination - a deeper understanding of oneself.

1. What are the achievements I am most proud of?

2. What are the values that guide my decisions?

3. What are the things I would like to improve about myself?

4. What are the biggest challenges I have faced, and how did I overcome them?

5. What are the things that make me happy?

6. What are my short-term and long-term goals?

7. How do I handle stress and setbacks?

8. What are the things I am grateful for?

9. How do I react to criticism?

10. What are the changes I can make to improve my life?

11. How do I handle failure and what lessons have I learned from it?

12. What are the most important relationships in my life and why?

13. How do my actions align with my values?

14. How do I balance my personal and professional life?

15. What motivates me in life?

16. How have my experiences shaped who I am today?

17. What does success mean to me?

18. How do I handle change?

19. What are the most significant changes I've experienced in my life?

20. How do I define personal success?

21. What role does self-care play in my life?

22. How have my failures contributed to my growth?

23. How do I maintain my physical and mental health?

Now that you have these questions to help you get started, there are few factors which are important to implement before, starting reflection for an effective and positive outcome.

Initiating the process of self-reflection is a personal journey that should begin when one feels ready. It's not something that can be imposed or rushed. Individuals vary in their levels of self-awareness.

For instance, those with high self-awareness often find self-reflection to be a natural and effortless process. I, for one, fall into this category. However, there are others who may struggle with self-reflection due to lower levels of self-awareness."

There are several ways to enhance your self-reflection skills, one of which is *journaling*. This practice can help you understand yourself better and process your thoughts, emotions, and goals in a healthier and more effective way. When thoughts and feelings are written down, they can be viewed more objectively, almost from a different perspective, as you're not consumed by the emotions and thoughts at that moment."

Consider an old photograph. Trying to recall the details from memory can be vague, especially as time passes and life moves forward. It's natural that you might not remember every detail accurately. However, when you hold that photo in your hands, the details become clearer and the memory is more vivid because nothing is interfering with it. Similarly, journaling can provide a clearer and more precise record of your thoughts, feelings, and experiences than relying on internal reflection alone.

Examine your emotional reaction, is another way, which can help you with your self-reflection. By paying attention to how you react to different situations, you can enhance your self-awareness. Every reaction is a response to an action or experience. These reactions, particularly the emotions they evoke, can trigger introspective questions. This process can open your mind to self-reflection, helping you understand yourself better."

Being gentle with yourself is essential in self- reflection process, "Being gentle with oneself is crucial in the process of self-reflection. Everyone has a unique journey and varying levels of emotional intelligence. Self-reflection is a personal growth journey, and it's important to recognize oneself as an individual. If you're hard on yourself, it can create mental and emotional blockages and even physical discomfort. When you encounter a thought or feeling that seems too difficult, or you feel like you can't do it, or you question the point of it all, remember to take deep breaths in through your nose and out through your mouth. Do this a few times until you start to feel relaxed. Of course, you can also engage in other activities like housework, errands, or spending time with friends. Sometimes, the more we try to force something, the less effective it becomes. At times, all you need is to let go and not think about it, and the insight will come naturally."

Mindfulness is a technique that can be learned and practiced. While some people might naturally be more present in the moment, mindfulness is a skill that can be developed over time. It involves training your mind to focus on the present moment and accept it without judgment. There are many ways to cultivate mindfulness, such as through meditation, yoga, or simply paying more attention to your daily activities. There are also numerous resources available, including books, online courses, and apps, that can guide you in learning and practicing mindfulness.

Whether you choose to explore journaling, mindfulness, or any other method that aids in self-reflection and personal growth, the goal is a happier, more tranquil you. It's crucial to maintain a sense of calm and openness as you try new strategies, seeking the ones that resonate most with you. Remember, these skills require practice, time, patience, and determination. **Progress at your own pace, and in time, you will master these skills.**

LIFE LESSONS FROM FAMOUS PEOPLE

In this illuminating chapter, we delve into the wisdom imparted by some of the world's most renowned figures. Each individual has left an indelible mark on the tapestry of human history. Their experiences, triumphs, and even their failures, serve as valuable lessons for us. As we explore these famous lessons from famous people, we invite you to not just read, but to reflect and learn. May their insights inspire you, challenge you, and guide you in your own journey. Welcome to a treasure trove of timeless wisdom.

Steve Jobs: "Don't be afraid to be different." Steve Jobs was never afraid to be different. He embraced being different and ended up making millions because of his unique business approach.

Oprah Winfrey: "The life you want begins by embracing the life you have." Accept and appreciate the life you have. Do not keep looking at the future wishing you had more, this way you miss what is good about your life already.

Nelson Mandela: "All people are equal and therefore deserving of basic respect and dignity." To be a great leader in any field, be it work or in your daily life, you need to treat all people with respect. All people are equal no matter their race, class or gender.

John Lennon: "Life is what happens to you while you're busy making other plans." If you are always so busy making plans for tomorrow, this weekend, next month or next year it is easy to let today slip through your hands.

Marilyn Monroe: "Sometimes things fall apart so that better things can fall together." These wise words from one of the most iconic women in history can help us through tough times.

Winston Churchill: "A pessimist sees the difficulty in every opportunity; an optimist sees the opportunity in every difficulty." This famous quote from Winston Churchill contains an essential life lesson.

George Washington: "Focus on the work, not the prize." In the wake of the Continental army's triumph over the British, Washington could have accepted glory and lavish titles.

WISDOM ECHOES

Insights: You'll gain insights into the lives of renowned figures and the wisdom they've imparted. These insights span across various aspects of life, including personal growth, leadership, creativity, perseverance, and more.

Life Lessons: The experiences and stories of these famous individuals provide valuable life lessons. These lessons can help you navigate your own journey, offering guidance and inspiration when you need it most.

Reflection: This chapter encourages reflection, allowing you to not only read about these lessons but also to think about how they apply to your own life.

Inspiration: The wisdom of these famous individuals can serve as a source of inspiration, motivating you to strive for success, overcome challenges, and make a positive impact in your own way.

INSIGHTS

In the journey of life, we often look for signposts that guide us towards the right path. These signposts come in the form of insights that we gain from the experiences of others. Renowned figures from various walks of life have left behind a treasure trove of wisdom that they've gleaned from their own journeys. These insights span across various aspects of life, including personal growth, leadership, creativity, perseverance, and more. They serve as a guiding light, illuminating our path and helping us make informed decisions.

LIFE LESSONS

Every individual's life is a unique story, filled with experiences that teach valuable lessons. The lives of famous individuals are no different. Their experiences, both good and bad, serve as life lessons for us. These lessons, distilled from their successes and failures, triumphs and tribulations, can help us navigate our own journey. They offer guidance when we're lost, inspiration when we're low, and wisdom when we're in doubt.

REFLECTION

Reflection is a powerful tool that allows us to learn from these insights and life lessons. This chapter encourages you to not only read about these lessons but also to think about how they apply to your own life. Reflection helps us internalize these lessons, understand their relevance, and apply them in our own unique circumstances. It's a process of introspection that helps us grow as individuals and make better decisions.

INSPIRATION

The wisdom of these famous individuals can serve as a source of inspiration. Their stories of resilience in the face of adversity, of determination in the pursuit of their goals, and of success achieved through hard work and perseverance, can motivate us to strive for success in our own way. They inspire us to dream big, to overcome our challenges, and to make a positive impact in our own unique way.

RESILIENCE: THE JOURNEY TOWARDS SELF-RELIANCE

1. Personal Fulfillment: Pursuing your dreams brings a sense of accomplishment and satisfaction. It gives your life purpose and direction, making every effort worthwhile.

2. Overcoming Obstacles: The path to your dreams is often filled with obstacles. These challenges test your resolve and resilience. Overcoming them not only brings you closer to your dreams but also strengthens your character.

3. The Value of Support: The support of loved ones can be a powerful motivator. It provides emotional strength and encouragement when the journey gets tough. However, it's important to remember that the ultimate responsibility for achieving your dreams lies with you.

4. Self-Reliance: There may be times when you have to forge ahead without external support. This is where self-reliance comes into play. Believing in yourself, backing your abilities, and being your own cheerleader are crucial for success.

5. The Pursuit of Happiness: Ultimately, following your dreams is about seeking happiness and peace. It's about creating a life that aligns with your values and aspirations. The struggles and sacrifices are worth it if they lead to a fulfilling and contented life.

6. Personal Growth: The journey towards your dreams offers numerous opportunities for personal growth. You learn new skills, gain new experiences, and develop a better understanding of yourself and the world around you.

BOOK SUMMARY AND CLOSING STATEMENT

This book is a collection of life lessons and important messages drawn from my personal experiences, perspectives, and the wisdom of renowned figures. It was crucial for me to include diversity, reflecting the rich tapestry of human experiences and wisdom.

The book traverses' various aspects of life, offering insights into personal growth, leadership, creativity, perseverance, and more. It encourages reflection, providing you with the opportunity to not only read about these lessons but also to contemplate how they apply to your own life.

The wisdom echoed in this book serves as a source of inspiration, motivating you to strive for success, overcome challenges, and make a positive impact in your own unique way. It's a testament to the power of seizing the moment, embracing self-love, and living life to the fullest. However, it's important to note that the aim of this book is not to dictate how you should live your life. Instead, it's about sharing experiences and knowledge that might resonate with you. The decision to implement these lessons is entirely up to you. They are offered as potential tools for you to navigate your own journey.

I hope that you have found this book insightful and helpful. My sincere wish is that the wisdom and experiences shared within these pages will inspire you, guide you, and empower you in your own journey of life.

AUTHOR'S NOTE

Writing this book has been a deeply fulfilling journey for me. As someone who is intellectual, philosophical, and spiritual, and as a motivational speaker, I have always believed in the power of words and ideas to inspire and transform lives.

While many motivational speakers use their voice to spread their message, I have chosen to use my hands to write this book. This has been my way of reaching out to you, of sharing my insights and experiences, and of hopefully making a positive impact on your life.

Each word I've written is a part of me, a reflection of my thoughts, my beliefs, and my experiences. It's my hope that these words will resonate with you, inspire you, and perhaps even help you navigate your own journey.

Remember, this book is not about telling you how to live your life. It's about sharing experiences and knowledge that might resonate with you. The decision to implement these lessons is entirely up to you. They are offered as potential tools for you to navigate your own journey.

I hope that you have found this book insightful and helpful. My sincere wish is that the wisdom and experiences shared within these pages will inspire you, guide you, and empower you in your own journey of life.

Thank you for joining me on this journey. It has been an Honor and a privilege to share my insights with you.

THE JOURNEY CONTINUES

As we come to the end of this book, it's important to remember that the journey of learning and growth never truly ends. Each day presents new opportunities for us to learn, to grow, and to become better versions of ourselves. The wisdom echoed in this book is meant to serve as a guide, but the journey is ultimately yours to embark on.

I have enjoyed every moment of writing this book. It has been a journey of self-discovery, of introspection, and of growth. I have learned so much about myself and about life in the process. And I hope that in reading this book, you too have gained valuable insights and learned important life lessons.

FINAL THOUGHTS AND FUTURE PROJECTS

In conclusion, I want to express my deepest gratitude to you, the reader. Thank you for taking the time to read this book, for embarking on this journey with me, and for allowing me to share my insights and experiences with you.

I would also like to mention that a lot of thought has been put into the design of the book cover. I believe that the cover is just as important as the content of the book. It's the first thing you see, and it sets the tone for the rest of the book. In my books, you will not only find the story within the pages but also the story behind the book cover.

As we close this chapter, I am excited to share that this is just the beginning. My aim is to continue empowering and inspiring you through my work. As a known non-fiction writer, I am committed to creating works that not only inform but also enlighten, educate, and inspire.

THE JOURNEY AHEAD

Looking ahead, I am filled with anticipation and excitement for the journey that lies before us. I have several future projects lined up that I am very excited about. These projects will delve deeper into the themes we've explored in this book, offering new perspectives and insights. My hope is that these future works will continue to serve as a source of inspiration and empowerment for you.

A PERSONAL NOTE

On a personal note, I want to say that writing this book has been one of the most rewarding experiences of my life. It has allowed me to reflect on my own journey, to share my insights and experiences, and to connect with readers like you. I am deeply grateful for this opportunity and I look forward to continuing this journey with you in my future works.

THANK YOU

Once again, I want to express my heartfelt thanks to you, the reader. Your support and engagement mean the world to me. I hope that you have found this book insightful and helpful, and that it has inspired you in some way. Remember, life is a journey, not a destination. So, keep moving forward, keep learning, keep growing, and most importantly, keep living. Because at the end of the day, life is meant to be lived, not just understood.

ABOUT THE AUTHOR

Kristina Alavanja, born in the picturesque city of Zadar, Croatia, she has been loving In South Australia since early teens where she has been living since her early teens.

In "Inspirational and Empowering: A Holistic Journey", Kristina shares her personal reflections on life's lessons and the path to growth. This book is not just a collection of theories, but a holistic insight into people's lives, complete with years of her journey through personal experience. It offers insights into the complexities of life and how we can seek wisdom that uplifts.

Kristina believes in the transformative power of words and uses them to provide healing, motivation, and inspiration. Her book offers a practical collection of affirmations, insights, and statements that can uplift the heart and highlight the silver lining. With the right mindset, she believes we can fulfill our dreams and live happily.

Her passion for inspiring people through writing has made her a beacon of change. She wants us to look back at the future and hopes to continue this journey, potentially touching even more lives through her future writings.

ACKNOWLEDGMENTS

First and foremost, I would like to express my deepest gratitude to my family. Your unwavering love and support have been my anchor in the stormiest of seas. I have learned so much from all of you, both directly and indirectly, and I am eternally grateful to have you in my life. Thank you for always believing in me and for being there for me during my darkest times. I love you all.

I am especially thankful to my mother, who is my idol and my inspiration. She is a woman of wisdom, intelligence, grace, and beauty. A woman who has survived the hardest parts of her life with strength and courage. She is the bravest person I know and she is my light and my strength in this life. In times when life gets too dark, she is the one who pulls me back into the light.

To my dear readers, I sincerely hope that you all have someone like that in your lives. Someone who inspires you, supports you, and loves you unconditionally.

ADDITIONAL ACKNOWLIDGEMENT

In addition to my family, I would like to acknowledge the profound impact that my professional experiences as a counsellor and coach have had on my journey. These roles have provided me with unique insights into the human experience, inspiring me to delve deeper into the themes explored in this book.

Every individual I have had the privilege to guide and support has taught me something valuable. Their stories, their struggles, their triumphs, and their resilience have enriched my understanding of life and its complexities. I am deeply grateful for these experiences and for the lessons I have learned from them.

Moreover, life itself has been a great teacher. The experiences I've had, the challenges I've faced, and the obstacles I've overcome have all shaped me into the person I am today. They have instilled in me a sense of empathy and understanding that I hope is reflected in my writing.

In my journey as a counsellor and coach, I have met nine individuals whose strength, resilience, and desire to heal from past trauma and improve self-love have been thoroughly inspiring. Their ability to take control over their lives and look forward instead of back, even in the darkest moments, has been a testament to the indomitable human spirit. I am so honoured to have been a part of their journey. Their trust in me has been as precious as a drop of water in a desert, a symbol of hope and faith.

This experience has shown me that no matter what we go through and how hard we are on ourselves, if we truly want something, we can achieve it. It's a powerful reminder of our capacity for change and growth.

It's a testament to human resilience and determination. No matter the challenges we face or the self-doubt we may experience, if we have a clear goal and a strong desire, we can achieve what we set out to do. This is indeed a powerful reminder of our capacity for change, growth, and personal development. It's important to keep this in mind as we navigate through life's ups and downs..

Don't miss out!

Visit the website below and you can sign up to receive emails whenever Kristina Alavanja publishes a new book. There's no charge and no obligation.

https://books2read.com/r/B-A-PDKAB-NTVXC

BOOKS 2 READ

Connecting independent readers to independent writers.